DEEPFAKE SERENADE

DEEPFAKE SERENADE
CHRIS BANKS

NIGHTWOOD EDITIONS

2021

Nightwood Editions
P.O. Box 1779
Gibsons, BC VON 1VO
Canada
www.nightwoodeditions.com

COVER ART: Anthony Hurd
COVER DESIGN: Carleton Wilson
TYPOGRAPHY: Carleton Wilson

Nightwood Editions acknowledges the support of the Canada Council for the Arts, the
Government of Canada, and the Province of British Columbia through the BC Arts Council.

This book has been produced on 100% post-consumer recycled, ancient-forest-free paper,
processed chlorine-free and printed with vegetable-based dyes.

Printed and bound in Canada.

LIBRARY AND ARCHIVES CANADA CATALOGUING IN PUBLICATION

Title: Deepfake serenade / Chris Banks.
Names: Banks, Chris, 1970- author.
Description: Poems.
Identifiers: Canadiana (print) 20210244909 | Canadiana (ebook) 20210244925 |
    ISBN 9780889714106 (softcover) | ISBN 9780889714113 (HTML)
Classification: LCC PS8553.A564 D34 2021 | DDC C811/.6—dc23

for Aura

It is hard to mix emotion and sincerity with irony and distance.

.– Stephen Dobyns

Contents

Deepfake Serenade

Children's laughter is like a spray of confetti
without the sweep of the broom afterwards.
Bodies are wiring. Love is the circuit. Houses
are constructed without balconies, lessening
the risk of serenades and therefore early deaths.
Inside every one of us is a deepfake. A holy ghost.
Folk tales led me to believe people find gold
only to lose it all the time. Each kiss is fourteen-carat.
How did I become exiled in a land of golden arches?
To push desire beyond the outwardness of roses
is to feel thorns. I am sorry to be serenading you
like this in a courtyard. Not a courtyard
but at night. Maybe not night either,
though it is true we just met. Forgive me,
I killed your cousin and your parents hate mine.
Don't think I wasn't shocked to discover
after climbing this wall of air between us
our elopement is a no go. Turns out
our stars are not crossed so much as shining
in separate hemispheres. Well, here is
to serenading exquisite strangers anyways!
Thank you for sealing my fate. Now let us go
before the guards make their final rounds.
Sadly, we all die in the final act.

Reverse

Conquistadors sail back to Spain,
leaving the Amazon untouched.
An old man regains his memories,
a child her innocence. The giant oak
overhanging the street is an acorn
with mighty ideas. The marriage
never happens because *I love you*s
slip backwards into the lovers' mouths.
How runs the stream? Strange to think
of time running opposite. Hindsight
in front of you like a coxswain telling you
to pick up the pace as you row
toward old tragedies and delights.
Maybe you will handle things differently
this time. The dead dog is a puppy
in your arms. Your deceased friend
smiles. The cancer cells gone. Despite
the creams, you are getting younger
and younger looking. Where does it end?
With no surprises. Tomorrow is already
yesterday. Perhaps it is best time runs on
ahead of us, the past a guide, and not a bully
waiting up the path, taking off his rings
one by one, saying this is going to hurt.
I guess I will take the future even if it means
our lives unravel unknown like red carpets
at a debutante ball where fate is only a minor
player at the party in a tuxedo handing out
pickled hors d'oeuvres. The rest of us
look for dance partners, or maybe leave early,
because lost as we are, at least we are moving

the way sharks do not stop moving,
the days, the hours, the minutes,
wild, unfamiliar, free.

Pleasures of the Authentic

I feel most times like an Edward Gorey character
pulled from an illustration, made to stand here
among the traffic lights and the mall renovations.
Just the mere act of living one day at a time now
a diminishment of all the romantic possibilities
I dreamed of in my twenties. No one ever dies
of ennui. At least you can hit two or three words
together to spark a new idea or a conceit but
I've grown too old to explain how images work
to the young. The world happens with or without
you. The tree in my yard will be standing long
after I'm gone. A poem persists whether anyone
reads it or not. In Montreal, I remember long
winters, my own inability to write anything
but failure, which reduced me to reading and
rereading the work of others who were like gods
to me, the way their poems flowed through,
eddied around forms, a consciousness that
seemed semi-divine but really was the product
of hard work and ambition. You can't teach
ambition, which is the pilot light of any poem.
Mostly, I want more from a meagre lifetime
of teaching which is why I catch a glimpse of
my former self scurrying down Saint Urbain Street
with the snow falling lightly on iron staircases
of the many houses while I try to find my way
to the graduate party where I will no doubt
be embraced by friends. I remember the lights
lining the street, the warm glow coming out
of the houses, my trudging along sidewalks
through snow, thinking life does not get

better than this, this soft sifting of memory
and experience, which itself is like a Gorey
illustration, the tiny figure in the foreground,
the houses looming about him, a stirring
of menace somewhere in the frame. I'm forty-
seven, and I still love that kid who will not
know addiction for at least ten more years.
The way his life is still unwritten. His only
thought whether to pick up a quart of beer
from the depanneur where a twelve-year-old
boy sits smoking beside his grandfather, or
whether to pick up bagels on the way home.
I'm hungry for that life but I can touch it
in a poem.

Love Hotel Republic

When leaves begin to fall, I think of the whiff
of old books. How the season marks us down,
remaindered, underappreciated, overwhelmed,
humiliated by the mere fact of our humanness,
despite luxuries like French poetry, daylight
saving time, full-body massages. The heart
a republic of love hotels, satin sheets, erotic
frescoes, sweet nothings. Even if love
is a ghost, see-through, otherworldly, I crave
its perpetual return. How it sails into our lives,
fading out, then materializing, always there
at the right moment, a few casual words spoken
between two people who suddenly find
themselves like two tired explorers reaching
some destination together. Love was the voice
we had before we had voices. I often remember
every moment of desolation in the times
between love. A feeling of baffled loneliness
live-streaming days and nights as if it were
in style to be sad. To feel apart. Love is both
symptom and synonym. How the spirit world
enters our bodies, makes our limbs rhyme. It
spins the loom of desire. A flagon of cinnamon
hearts and pheromones. Today the leaves fall,
a translation of last year's season appearing new,
which makes me think of love coming again
this late in life, not as a credo, or as an announcement,
but as a returning season, one never ending.

Male Ego

Little caged animal growling in my rib cage,
telling me I am so much more than stardust,
interstellar debris, living mud, holy atoms,
I refuse to feed you any longer. The way
you try to mansplain history. The world
no longer a comfortable nest, but a vessel
of competing ideologies, other voices.
You are bad at sharing toys. You brag
about running with bulls, yet live in
a china shop, cry at the drop of a plate.
Even your therapist is sick of the self-pity,
the endless *poor me* stories. She suggests
writing a letter to yourself, but you pull out
a mirror instead. You become unhinged
when others talk about your need to find
a feminine side. Your cologne sends
people to opposite ends of the room.
The things you seek end in conquest.
You wonder why you have no friends.
Little animal, Jurassic hunger, your eon
was all hand-grip strength, chest-bumping,
but we've reached a tipping point. Stop
shining Little League trophies. Pamper
others until you like pampering others.
There is nothing more grandiose than
learning the cage is of your making.

Tragedy

A groom dies in a crash on the way
to his wedding. A toddler is killed
by a falling tree on a school field trip
to the Botanical Gardens. Tragedy waltzes
into your personal space, slowly drapes
an arm around the small of your back,
dances you around its fields of waste
until you feel sick. Dizzy from lost
potential. I hate child deaths the most.
News-cycle stories about little kids
drowning in rivers, getting torn apart
by dogs, wandering out a front door
at night, dying of exposure to winter.
Tragedy says, *Have a nice day. I'll see
you around.* Claps you on a shoulder,
leaving a bloody handprint behind.
Even when hope sails the horizon,
a little white boat riding the curve
of the Earth, wave upon lazy wave,
Tragedy starts a fire in the engine
room, or hoists a black flag instead
of a white one, so someone jumps
off a cliff, thinking their only son
is dead but is really alive, just a jerk
who does not know how to treat
a lady right. Tragedy is the promise
of unhappy endings. The hint of
one's own demise. Its guidance system
does not discriminate, targets young
and old, rich and poor, tears a hole
in the perfect story, multiplies pain,

anguish exponentially. It is the drone
you don't see until the bomb hits,
the flash and panic and human losses
exactly what it is designed to do.

Memorandum

The moon is moving measurably
away from the Earth every year.
In space, you do not cry because
there is no gravity to make tears flow.
Not sure this has anything to do
with 1,800 thunderstorms sprawling
over oceans and continents at any
given time. I learned most lipstick
contains fish scales. To testify
derives from a Roman practice of
making men swear on their testicles.
Coca-Cola was originally green,
a detail sparking neurons in my brain
to fire two hundred times per second,
when really all I wanted to say
was something nice about flowers,
like how tulips were once a form
of currency, or how their bulbs
can be substituted for onions,
which are stray facts sitting in
a surgical tray until I place them
here for safekeeping. So what?
The truth is most facts will never
give me a night's satisfaction, no
matter what I say about Leonardo
da Vinci inventing scissors,
roller coasters being first designed
to help people avoid sin, Buzz
Aldrin urinating on the lunar
surface. No wonder the moon
is moving away from us! This is

a memorandum of understanding
between me and Voyager I spinning
its golden record way out past
our solar system, Mozart playing
in the vacuum of space, as if
in its data stream, its little sighs
of ones and zeros, there might be
an official important message,
and not just a random assortment of facts
calling collect to the stars
that have no answering machines.

Oracle

Be prepared for sons and daughters

to overthrow you at dusk's picnic.

The wound will not be staunched by

money or Aristotle. You will stand

for the national anthem. Levitation

is not your forte. There will be times

when it is impossible to tell any

difference between bad omens or iffy

emotions hiding behind barriers of

speech. You are sad. You are funny.

Unravelling hints to the future takes

time. Know your limits. The dream

states the new will overtake the old.

The random the linear. Make your

words count. Be more than a vessel

of secrets. A primer of wrong turns.

Those three crows eating a roadside

carcass have something to do with

your feelings. I am a liar who plays

to the masses. You will bear grudges

against a family member. You will

stand under the colossi of many stars

thinking them small vowels of light.

The prophecy will be recognized in

a lover's arms. Its birth notice made

in the estrangement of the past. Be

patient, for your destiny lies beyond

the confines of any page, signs are

automatic, a cat's purr, a sunflower's

bloom, a stone's heft, the messages,

the acute details, yours to interpret.

Avatar, Sweet Avatar

This is the year of living hermetically sealed inside houses,
away from each other. Away from monarch butterflies
and neighbourhood ponds and calculus formulas. The world
was a better place when there was more doo-wop in songs,
more astronauts orbiting the moon, which is saying something
since that time had its share of riots and marches and villages
on fire. My parents no longer wonder where I am at dusk.
The theme of this school prom sucks. Who chose *A Quarantine
to Remember*? You lose things aging like barns full of teenagers
dancing to "Rock Lobster" by the B-52s. Still plenty of Mark Rothko
paintings and Hubble Telescope pictures to go around though.
Too much of my life involves little Allen keys and obsessing
about takeout. I try to put the pieces together, but inevitably
I am missing something. I am tired of being mostly water
when I want to be mostly cloud looking down on the messes
we have made. I need to take my anxiety for a walk. To
decommission my ghosts. I am sure there is a podcast to feel
like I am lost inside a forest when the forests are all gone.
I miss the Hare Krishnas the Jehovah's Witnesses killed.
Even hummingbirds are dying this summer from poisoned
sugar water. Ziploc hate. Crowdfund love. STEM is cool
but have you tried the arts? If we could just translate what
the flowers have been saying for millennia, without any
extra improvised words, we could solve world peace
with chrysanthemums and not batons. Says who? Says
the cynic in me holding hands with the cynic in you.
After half a century of trying to understand light, it is clear
I am not going to get the bonus question on the exam.
I wish I knew the secret password, but it is in a dialect only
the rain speaks. Oh, and crows! No salve for the rational,
unfortunately. I am smart and funny and although this is not

a race, I am losing it anyways. A fracas of figments is how
I explain the noise of my thinking. How about a photo finish
between myself, the river, everything in between? I smashed
all the lamps inside words, but still connections shine through.
It is hard to get my bearings when late emergencies arrive.
My avatar is a siren. My epitaph lies between the advertisement
for sea monkeys and the one for X-ray specs: *Be of use.*

Daffodils

*When I think of all the good times I've wasted
having good times* is the happenstance truth of
my twenties and thirties. Being no more than
a serf to a beer bottle is no way to save on
human suffering or the virtues of marriage.
I love the movie *Big Fish*. Ewan McGregor
standing in a field of yellow daffodils.
Something I long to do, for whatever scent
they give off is sure to rid me of any wish
to be understood. Notice I didn't mention
Wordsworth, who was a great lover of daffodils,
turning into the canon? *Quit all this nonsense
and buy the Early Bird Special,* says the diner's
billboard. My highlight reel keeps me up all
night. Yesterday banishes me. The past tucks you
in at bedtime, or else beats you in the woods
with a phone book. Loss is more than bruises.
A handful of syllables. Our prophets auto-tune
insipid pop songs as we enter this next round
of extinction. I rent my memoirs by the hour,
but tomorrow is still a work in progress. Even
when there are no words, I mumble a few *ifs*
to keep me going until the next sea change.
Already the little black box of consciousness
is readying itself for some crash landing. Wait
for the heart to uncross itself. I believed in
immortality until the sky gaslighted me with
arguments of rain. When shall we meet again?
I'll be inventorying olive trees and butterflies,
standing in a field of daffodils waiting for you.
I'll be here until beauty changes the locks.

Show and Tell

I have this birthmark on my forearm. A copy of Lorca's
"Gacela of the Dark Death" on my office door. I share
twenty-two pairs of chromosomes with my favourite poets,
making us family. My soul feels snagged on my insides
like an empty plastic bag caught on a branch in winter.
Here is my white flag surrendering my position. All
the heads on Easter Island have bodies buried beneath
the ground. The moon has moonquakes. My body
emits light, but not enough to stumble a path without
a torch at night. Even pigeons can tell the difference
between a Monet and a Picasso so what is your excuse?
Outer space smells like seared steak. Show and tell
felt more fun in grade school. Yet here I am standing
at the front of the classroom saying I have enough iron
in my blood to produce a nail three inches long. Koalas
have fingerprints. Saturn and Jupiter rain diamonds.
Here is a letter I wrote to Jacques Cousteau when I was
young. Here is a dissection tray full of failed relationships.
Despite me not being a scientist, here is my laboratory
where I mix cardiac tremors with a field of sunflowers
recording the results. Maybe I am doing this all wrong
because the dog I brought to class on a leash is a wolf.
This map of stars I unfurled is really only target paper
peppered with BB gun pellets. Think of these broken
guitar strings and worn lacy garters as my Declaration
of Interdependence. When people ask you to show them
who you really are, tell them about your Yellow Pages
of found objects, your penchant for strange facts—
how crows hold grudges, how sharks existed before
trees, how there is a jellyfish that is immortal—
and maybe they will put a gold star, a little token,
a little ballyhoo beside your name.

My Report to the United Nations

for Aura

Forty thousand scientists cannot be wrong,
so why are we lining up for lattes? Throwing
batteries in garbage bins? Weren't we raised in
social science classes? We pretend the world's
obsession with disaster porn has little to do
with a global coffee shortage in twenty years,
or the oceans rising to the Statue of Liberty's
midriff. Arctic shelves melting into oblivion.
The stock markets are booming. The dog
needs a walk. Children are calling for a snack
so we throw another single-use plastic bottle
into the recycling, then get on with this living
which has something to do with tenderness,
with putting arms around shoulders, with
kissing you so intensely you feel for a moment
surrounded by a rainforest when in reality
the actual rainforest is burning, the last
undiscovered tropical bird beating its wings
against the flames. Maybe the kiss is worth it.
Maybe we should sit and enjoy the marching
band as it passes us by, not thinking about
whether or not the Gulf Stream will turn off
triggering a mini ice age, or whether there
will be houses or free health care for our kids
when they have stopped running with scissors
and are old enough to vote. I know, I know.
I'm colouring outside the lines. I'll never be
anyone's Poet of the Month. Kiss me again.
Tell me I'm sexy. Maybe we can be together

a few decades longer, go to Greece, me still
handsome, just older, you stepping out of
the Mediterranean, the sun's golden floss
in your hair, as hand in hand we play
Red Rover with the future, except
neither of us are children anymore,
as the last undiscovered tropical bird
cries somewhere beyond the horizon.

Grand Scale

You have to leave Earth. Talk about Orion's Belt
having the brightest stars like you spent a holiday
orbiting Betelgeuse once. Mention Ancient Egypt.
Note their belief Osiris would return from Orion
then admit you cannot see the stars for the roof
over your head. Zoom into minutiae. Confess
how you stole a book from a friend's bathroom
at a party in your twenties, then spent the whole
next day reading the book before apologizing
and giving it back. The poem of the grand scale
needs you to mention echolocation. How sperm
whales and dolphins use sonar to stun their prey.
Dark stirrings at the bottom reaches of oceans.
But next it wants to talk about your vasectomy.
The fact you cannot have any more children, even
though you have two wonderful kids with an ex
who still talks to you, and anyways, it isn't really
interested in more children. It just likes the idea
of birth. And strangeness. It talks about strangers.
Like the old Asian man in your neighbourhood in
the blue jumpsuit who does walking meditation
backwards every morning as you drive to work.
He could be you. Or me. It is seductive, the poem
of the grand scale. The sense of walking backwards
through life, zooming through space, plumbing
the depths of oceans. It wants you to believe
everything is connected. That everything aligns
with the stars. That although the pantry is bare,
the shelves are full, if only we took time to look.

Honeydripper

God's voice is the sound of a modem connecting
to a rose bush. A volcano sending a fax of lava.
Divinity is a kid pouring either honey or gasoline
over ant nests. My signature embarrasses me:
I still make a little circle over the *i* like I did
in grade school. Serial killers are getting their own
television channel even though their universe
is essentially a house painted black full of human
skulls. I like spontaneity. A little imagination.
Every new phrase, siren of syllables, is less
like a three-car pileup. More like a newborn child's
faint talcum whiff of the womb. "Rock-a-bye Baby"
is a horror story about innocence lost. A teen boy
wearing an *Obey* T-shirt is arrested by police.
Irony condemns him to a lifetime sentence.
My supply of mentors has been used up. I'm all out
of slogans and Johnny Cash lyrics to explain
where we go from here. I am tired—not from
holding the world up—from living in my body.
My neighbours are trying the latest fad diet.
You cut out sugar and carbs and gluten and people
who disagree with you. I tried to go metaphor-free
for a month but I ended up walking my dog
beside the million blue marbles of the river.
Revelations should come in hard copy. Crack
the spine. All my secrets spill out. If you are
not living your best life, bury it in a shallow grave.
Start over. Choose hummingbirds over Humvees.
Butterflies over blowtorches. Feel better about yourself
even if last picked. Stamped it. No erasies.

Anger Is an Energy

John Lydon, circa 1983, snarled lips,
grey suit, short orange spikes, issuing
a call to arms, rallying against Rick
Springfield pop, Cyndi Lauper faux-
punk. His philosophy *Anger Is an*
Energy an absolute truth in face of teen
bullying, school masses. In 1983, I hated
school, flaunted my anger like a shield
of rebellion, while my father flew across
the great northern expanse of Ontario
in a Twin Otter seaplane, hopping from
one reserve to another. Once he took
my mother, brother, me along to Round
Lake for a three-day fishing trip.
I remember standing outside the cabin
that doubled as a police headquarters.
A group of Indigenous boys gathered nearby
before one young man came down the hill
to look at my brother and me.
He was silent as he stood there, his eyes
passing over my face and my brother's,
before hitting me as hard as he could
then running back to his friends. This
was years before I understood anything
about institutional racism, land claims,
settler mentality. I felt only a small flare,
blossom of pain, then the shock of it,
not understanding what he understood
all too clearly, which was we lived in
different worlds. The wind was warm.
I tasted my blood. The moment ticked

into the past as my brother and I stood
in amazement, no one saying anything
as the boy's anger, what had curled up,
waited for the presence of strangers,
passed like an energy into all our lives.

Inkblots

I have measured out my life in K-Cups.
Please add snow shovelling, foreign wars,
daddy-long-legs, vowels to the list. Rain
fell yesterday like a ritual. My children
are scared of thunderstorms. A golden
retriever is missing says a flyer stapled
to a hydro pole. God is lost. Life feels
unscripted. I say *rivers, fauna, skyscraper,*
expecting my hands, my mind to gift-wrap
it all into meaning. My language is tired
of looking for a common denominator.
Behind every word, the sound of a hinge
opening. Behind things entering my eyes,
a bridge to understanding. Press an ear
to my chest to hear a hive of contradictions.
Honey is the essence of wildflowers. Blood
is the essence of life owed to a massive star
at the centre of our galaxy. I remember this
despite failing astrology class. Despite
passing a lie detector. The inkblots prove
I am a good person. Radio telescopes
probe the universe for mysterious chatter
like these sentences full of fundraisers and
flood waters, love and work retirements,
quasars and champagne. The art of living
is seeing each other beyond addictions
and condos. I have waited my whole life
to emanate a brightness. To wear a halo of
knowing. Outside phenomena and inside
impulses collide. I am the sparks flying.

Old Ideas

Bloodletting clinics keep on advertising
we carry an excess of black bile and sad
country songs. *Lunacy* comes from *lunar*.
Ancients believed full moons drove people
crazy when really parties were thrown on
bright nights. I don't know if birds carry
the souls of the departed to heaven. Bring
back mummification without pharaohs.
Virgin births. Augury. Bread and circuses.
Old ideas deserve a remix. The modern
is synonymous with purgatory. Is there
a pot of gold at the end of thirty years
of work? If not, there should be. Every
civilization has its share of angry gods.
I tried standing inside mysteries. They
kept demanding a human sacrifice.
Nothing like firecrackers and wind
chimes to chase away evil spirits. If
you break a mirror, knock on wood.
Make your life a folk tale. A red sunrise
means danger lies ahead, or a terrible
sunburn. A daily commute is a road
of trials. *You are the chosen one,* says
your beloved but still you need to clean
the toilets. *More art, less matter,* says the voice
from the wishing well. The thread of life
has been cut, stitched into your resemblance.
Wear a hole in it. Earn your rewards.

All Your Power

All the glaciers are retreating.

The tea leaves say diseases in ice

are waking up. This movie

will end badly. I want to stop

firing blanks at the alphabet.

Your mouth tastes like red wine.

I misdialled starlight, crescendos,

cells dividing, but here you are

making me feel young again!

Tell me your secret mission.

I will tell you mine. I'm late

for my heart attack. One day

you are a moon-faced teenager,

the next you have crow's feet.

Time smiles paring his nails

with a knife. What must I do

to get a telegram from an anthill?

Sorting the full and the empty

is a lonely job. I want to talk

dirty and whistle into eternity.

Tailgate the solstice with you.

We invented beauty so light

would have something to talk

about. I apologize. I botched

the translation. I won the prize.

The secret is saying *I love you*

and meaning it. The barricades

are down. The war is over.

Flag Ceremonies on the Moon

Night is the grave we rise from each morning.
My mother carefully attends her husband
who, day by day, is slowly forgetting her.
I would like to banish my fears of cancer
and heart attacks and spelling bees.
Somewhere, new galaxies are being born.
A black hole is swallowing a neutron star.
All my words I prop up like tent poles
where I shelter inside narrative. Or surprise.
Or manifestations of meaning. I don't mean
to be Janus-faced in the face of old dualisms—
earth, sky, boy, girl, good, evil—but
simply living demands you make sacrifices
like making love to ambiguity. Love and hate
two sides of the same blanket you place upon
a bed you set on fire before sleeping in it.
My stethoscope of perception I place against
my heart, and I hear a rainstorm, a little Cuban
merengue, a cat carrier of hissing egos,
a kinder, gentler universe. In the meantime,
I get older, fatter, wiser. I try to be a giver
and not a kleptomaniac hoarding my stolen haul
of active volcanoes, unearthed Roman graffiti,
snippets of memories like B-movie trailers
starring guilt, fear, redemption. What
is a man to do when he is staring down
the second half of his life? Be better. Be more.
Hide the facts. Take inventory. Bite one's thumb
at one's enemies. If they draw swords,
throw flowers at them. Not everyone gets to walk
on the moon. Even an astronaut planting a flag

in lunar dust secretly knows a helmet is a bad window
compared to the see-through walls of his eyes.

Middle Age

I hate the phrase. It was easier when
Death was a dark horse in a fallow field;
not a wolf at the front door. I have lived
over half of my life watching young men
grow old. They now sport polarized
sunglasses, wear hearing aids. They tell
the same stories, over and over, having
euthanized the bit parts. I wish I cared more
about employment rates, but honestly,
Chinese poets, bioluminescent jellyfish,
are more likely to assuage anxiety,
despair in me than jobs, jobs, jobs,
which makes me think of Bishop's line
rainbow, rainbow, rainbow
so now you understand me better,
even though everything is supposed to be
downhill from here, where I oscillate
between knowing and not knowing,
looking for dreams to fill up my medicine cabinet
instead of actual prescriptions,
ones I take to keep my face toward the sun,
from drinking not poison, but Diet Coke,
which in truth is the same thing.

Liar, Liar

I stopped praying as a child when it was clear
God was not going to give me superpowers.
I started praying as an adult when I was told
I would die a drunk unless I supplicated
to a higher power. Every day is so full of lies
I could stuff a bed mattress. A human body.
The world is warming up but we tell children
recycling is foolproof. Someone burns a pot roast
but we eat our portion anyways. The meat
is delicious. The lies are delicious. How easy
they roll off our tongues. *How are you? I'm fine.*
A lie. No one will lose any jobs. A lie.
You are not alone carrying a torch through
the labyrinth of your own skull. A lie.
At least someone gave you this thread and
a sword to slay monsters. Monsters are not real.
A lie. White lies are colourless. Translucent.
They float around us like pollen or angels.
We spread lies so as not to hurt each other
too much. The moral of "The Emperor's New Clothes"
is truth hurts too much. Nakedness is silly
but as real as it gets. I am hungry. I am happy.
Someday my parents will die and I will suffer.
I swoon when you take off your chemise.
These are not lies. The red snapper on the menu
is a lie, but not my desires. Not my needs.
What lead me through this world, room by room,
looking for you, with my pants on fire.

On Narrative

Some do not like it at all. Would have
you chase inspiration like bloodhounds
a hare, skirt the bogs of personal stories.
The past not even remembrances. More
a burned-out apartment with a few units
mercifully intact filled not with tenants,
but rumours. Tell us about the sun's red
skirts. Dusk's box of ashes. The delicate
pastel blur of a hummingbird's wings.
It reminds me of the first time I saw
Terry Gilliam's *Brazil*. Its haunting
soundtrack. The protagonist flying high
above a cloudscape in a winged suit of
shining armour. Huge pillars erupting
from the ground, blocking out blue skies,
creating a maze he must navigate to find
his dream girl. I saw it dozens of times.
The message life is more than drudgery,
mere work, conformity, irresistible to
eighteen-year-old me. It was sublime,
but already I have forgotten this poem
was not to be about me, was supposed
to be all clean line breaks, aesthetics,
images only. Every new idea, metaphor,
stumbling down the rickety mine shaft
to the vein of ore below. These lines
talk about the seamless elegance of fire,
street pigeons like grey sacks of sorrow,
a wallpaper's patterned hopelessness
without mentioning any inwardness,
stories that are personal, and add up

to nothing, like dreams. Sam escaping
in his mind to live with Jill in the country
at the end of *Brazil*. The interrogator
Jack Lint unsatisfied, stating, "He's gone."
Sam strapped to a chair in an empty
coal-fired power plant, his smile haunting
as the film's music, inescapable.

No Soliciting

I can't remember the combination lock
to civilization. I should climb more trees,
fly more kites to stay closer to my inner
child. My inner child eats all the cookies,
quietly points to a *No Soliciting* sign when
I come calling. In the 70s I wore flared
jeans, rode a banana-seat blue bicycle.
It was easier to be astonished as a child.
You were more aware of your heartbeat,
clouds catalyzing into fantastic shapes,
your inability to fly. The road looked
the same forward as it did backward.
Adulthood is carrying a bag of darkness
over a shoulder. Sometimes you stick
a hand in it. You pull out a summer spent
landscaping a golf course, a wedding photo,
a five-week stint in rehab for a drinking
problem. My inner child circling around me
on his blue bicycle says *What's for dinner?*
I tell him my knees feel the weather more
and more. That death is coming up the aisle
with her beverage cart and the plane will
eventually go down in flames. He smiles,
revving the little plastic motor sound
attached to his handlebars. He tries to do
a wheelie before disappearing forever
which reminds me I still cannot fly
no matter how much I wave my arms,
attached as I am to gravity's anvil,
to the past's dead weight, to the knowledge
every little thing won't let me go.

Mystery Stories

Winter with its terrible scowl, ragged cough,
has been acting suspicious. The interviewing
takes its toll. A piebald horse I fed carrots to
across a cedar-rail fence when I was twenty-two
is a red herring. Look at the evidence.
There are many suspects. The little birds
flying from a treeline across a vacant field,
then back again have something to hide. Clues
are coping mechanisms. Deep inside the night,
there is violence brewing. Morning arrives
with its hints, misdirections. A relative or friend
turns up dead, so we search for answers.
The river is charged with multiple drownings,
but gets off scot-free on a technicality. The wind
wipes down a crime scene. Eventually there is a break
in the case. The children confess to full innocence.
The sun leaves its fingerprints on everything
except shadows. A pattern begins to emerge amidst
a campfire's flames, a cluster of shopping carts
left abandoned in a vacant lot. The past is
a femme fatale the present warns you about.
The moment emerges when from your mouth
slips a solution, a denouement, a long-held truth,
a secret leading you back to the beginning,
to a small fallen leaf, the polished gleam of
a horse's eye, its alibi significant.

Optimism

Some days you forget despair's tractor pull
long enough to see some little boy go
Vroom vroom with a toy car. Joy is
invisible, everywhere, like microplastics
in drinking water. Sure, children are
in concentration camps, the rivers are
polluted, a work colleague gets some
horrible disease, but joy's rumble is felt
beneath what is rotten. Why is there
no god of optimism? Ancient rites
of happiness? That we are mostly quarks
and water, but still feel joy is a bona fide
miracle. Blood hymns in sunshine.
Joy plunges its little dagger of shivers
over and over, into our hearts. Joy is
the surprise, after the surprise, after
apocalyptic narratives. I'm for joy getting
its own Nobel Prize. Buy the stilettos,
the travertine countertops if it makes
you happy, the antique desks and DJ
equipment while there is still time. Look,
I built this joy out of my imagination.
It is full of gold lamé, peacock feathers,
even toy cars. *Vroom vroom.*

Footnotes

Smoking opium with hill tribes in northern Thailand,   45
interrogating ballerinas in famous Degas paintings,
never felt important enough to talk about until
my last breakdown. Depression is an unbreakable lease.[1]
Heaven is a pagoda filled with boring people
wearing silly hats. I'm trying to get to the source
of the matter. This has something to do with
the teacher's edition, the answer key ripped out,
replaced with honeybees on an extinction list,
coral bleaching, migrant caravans, overdoses.
These footnotes I dedicate to my future self.[2]
I need a pep talk of small planets (though I am not
one for documentation). Read the appendix
to understand the appeal of Céline Dion, moths
in poems, mindfulness tapes, Camille Claudel's
last thirty years in an insane asylum. Who am I kidding?
The fine print teaches you how to live,
until the front door comes crashing down,
until zip ties ensnare your wrists. When asked
your name, take the plea. Say *Anonymous*.[3]

---

1   File a restraining order against the classics.

2   Follow your calling, but never into an ambush.

3   Although the universe is bugged, continue to speak freely.

For Your Consideration

Sorry this love letter is written in blood.
Embossing feelings on white linen paper
makes people believe you are genuine.
The songs are all lost because the guitar
caught fire. I read the script ahead of time.
The ending involves floods and fires
and possibly food stamps. Protozoa
are not scared of the end of the world
so why should we be? I'm hoping God
hits a switch and we evolve in time.
My children buoy joy above despair.
The foundation of civilization is leaking
but look for the people with buckets.
My T-shirt says *One Man Renaissance.*
Trying is the best form of optimism.
How many different ways can I write
the word *helpless*? Or *happiness*? Or
love? I miss being ten years old, chewing
raw spearmint in a forest alone.
I miss sidewalk soju trucks in Seoul
during monsoon season, which is funny
since I no longer drink. The way you had
to hold your umbrella open even under
the tent to keep the rain from reaching
your clothes. The other side of the street
abstracted, lost in the deluge. Live
minnows came swimming in a glass
for each table. One time they were gone.
My friend Neal said solemnly under
his black umbrella that it would be better
if the little fishies were here. I agreed,

as I agree now. When the rain thwacks
down on you, there should be a reward.
Let's get lost in the downpour. Open
our mouths. Taste the plenty.

#MiddleClass

The rain keeps odd office hours. I feel like a Mayan ruin.
Hard to be Zen knowing in fifty years the sun will boil
the swimming pools dry. Nature is not housebroken.
The returns on metaphors and similes are competitive,
but everyone is too obsessed with words like *terrorist,*
male enhancement, property taxes, special discount to notice.
FedEx does not deliver oceans or birdsong. I wish loss
spoke a language other than fear. Optimism needs
a new roof. There is a hornets' nest under the front
porch. I'm stoked by the life force emanating from young
people sitting in parks. Happy are the landlords. The meek
shall inherit exhaustion. I feel we have taken a wrong turn
even though the cruise control is active. The phone rings.
No one ever answers. I admit it. It is becoming harder
and harder to think of a loon's call, or photons of light
ping-ponging off of everything when you are inundated
with flyers for Lasik surgery or Botox. Write the poems
or do not. May your bookbags be overflowing. One day
we will tell the children how we could afford housing,
dance classes, lavender bath bombs. I guess I am trying
to get the story half right, teetering as I am between despair
and hope. Why is everything for sale? *Even Paradise*
had a price tag, says the wind. *You break it, you pay for it.*

Ballistics Report

Judge me and I'll serve my sentence willingly
but not before trying to stage a mutiny first.
Increment by increment, the world implicates you
in a ballistics report. The hardest part
is turning yourself in for the bounty. Remember
your childhood? The lone toboggan hill that sat
at the end of your street? Remember teen years
spent in line for mug shots? The police station eerily
abandoned? Adulthood is sitting in a small upper room
with binoculars looking out a window. Press play on
the reel-to-reel tapes. Listen intently. The recording says
you should not have stolen a pig's heart in Science
in grade ten, placed it in that girl's locker. My spiritual
problem is I'm more blood than spirit. I'll take paradox
over fakery. You cannot live on revelations alone.
Let's really see each other in this moment, okay?
Even the big finish dissolves into new beginnings
after the applause dies down. The red curtain drops.
Proceed toward the exit. For God's sake, stop playing
autopsy with your past. Every bright moment
drifts through you, in real time, whispering,
You must change your life! My theory is we spend most
of our time looking for the right words like lost socks,
when really so much goes unsaid, despite our best
behaviour. Despite early check-in. A whistle blows.
The game is over. You win. You lose. A girl with
an *In Training* pin hands you a coffee out a window.
It doesn't matter whether you are there or not.

Inflight Magazine

My childhood treehouse is lost in sleep.
So what if I never see the moons of Jupiter?
We have become avatars of supplication.
I signed the treaty but the war rages on.
Who wears this crown of thorns for me?
Reboot the empire. Defrag the climate.
Slide the needle in, but please only vaccines.
The brochure says I can go to Las Vegas.
The inflight magazine advertises every sin.
I do not want a bigger penis, thank you.
It's time for a new car, a paradigm shift.
I'm thinking we should hold hands together.
Some will pray while others shall weep.
Can we love our children *and* the planet?
Plastic shrink-wraps the periodic table.
Helium is sadly a non-renewable resource.
Try rinsing facts off during a hot shower.
No more reality TV, but more reality.
Now that you have come this far, will you
come a little farther? Here, hold these flowers.
Tell me what has come between us. No tricks!
Let us read the *Acta Sanctorum* of ourselves.
I try not to desire anything for even a day
but then the word *full* whispers *emptiness*,
so I say *river, sky, father, mother, sunrise*,
until my head is brimming with syllables.
Check off the boxes for *together* and *alone*.
Send in the application fee. It will be processed
as soon as you give me the high sign.

Galapagos Islands

Inside every TV pilot is a blockbuster.

A happy wreck. When I was ten,
I wanted to go to the Galapagos Islands
to adopt a tortoise. I wanted to hitch
a ride with Jacques Cousteau. Now
I'm just happy if my fries are cooked
in beef tallow. I take the little book
over the toy every time. No, you cannot
substitute knowledge for all-you-can-eat.
Extinction is a motherfucker. I wish
to be as happy as a leashed goat I once met
on the way to Dairy Queen. Into each life
a little bylaw must fall. I found the alley
but what is the password? Transformation
has its costs. Manna is my comfort food.
After eating, you have to wait an hour
for the operating system to update.
How long can I keep this up? I wish joy
was as dependable as the one Chinese food
restaurant in every small town. Someone
made me prime minister of this life. In my house,
the walls are a small fortress of books.
I burned my dream journals. I got another
tattoo. Dispense with the advice and go
straight for the jugular: the Academy
will never accept you. Win your category anyways.
Practise your speech. When you hear
the music playing, it's time to stop talking.
Raise the trophy. Be the prize.

Mint Condition

It is hard to mix emotion and sincerity
with irony and distance, said a poet more
famous than I. Still, I follow the recipe.
I keep my uncomfortable feelings in
mint condition like comics in plastic bags
on the top shelf of my bedroom closet.
The pills I take to combat side effects
of other pills I take are writing a novel
called *Sense and Senselessness*. True story.
Yesterday is forever trending. Scientists
discover that fish on the Great Barrier Reef
sing a dawn chorus in technicolour.
When you run out of map similes, childhood
metaphors, what are you left with? The goods.
Figments are rent-to-own. Herald the news.
Live life in your own key. Substitute fries
for existentialism. Time to rebrand the ocean.
The moon. Twilight. The stars. Strangely,
I have no ghostwriters. Only ghosts.
Accident or revelation? Is it too much
to ask for both? Face it: details matter
in a poem or in a life. I've spent years
trying to put lightning on a leash. All
the climate change zealots I know drink
Starbucks. The world was easier to understand
when movies came on celluloid. Truly,
I'm an apocalypse virgin. I'm hoping
to slip a little wisdom past the censors
like a poem must begin in lava, end in cathedrals.
Orange pylons adorn my street this week.
There is a wish to be elsewhere. To go past them.

Hot-wire

I botched my relationship with what is real
after hot-wiring the lyric. I taught my voice
another voice. There are bodies along the trail
to the summit. One moment you are talking
about swans, the next the mind is a rusty
Tilt-a-Whirl full of screaming kids. You can't kill
the self, no more than the "I," but wrest control
from its hands. Go spelunking with amnesia.
Start a countdown. If you push the detonator,
remember the answer is kaboom! I would rather
put the unbidden under surveillance than trot out
memories one more time, but someone is making
walkie-talkie demands. That summer in Europe
is proof of life. The board of directors resolved that
it's okay to use syntax and line, but are deadlocked
on the striped thorax of a dragonfly. I've made a hole
in the self with a penknife. A light shines out of it
as does hope, disappointment, longing, convictions.
The self does not care how we feel about it. It is
the voice banging on the other side of the door.
The burning bush laying down commandments
before someone douses it with a bucket of water.
The days are in charge, for now, but the nights
are plotting regime change. The self sharpens
its guillotine, fears the rabble in the streets.
It writes a pamphlet. Uses various pseudonyms.
After being caught in a police dragnet, it looks
down the long table, confesses to everything.
It implicates me. A sad crash test dummy.
See these two wires? Twist them together.
Hit the ignition. Let's make our getaway.

Escapism Is Fabulous

I am trying to sieve a few epiphanies
from palatial glass skyscrapers, sunspots,
microwave ovens, fake antiques, honeybees
nuzzling yellow stamens, daily clickbait,
a thousand poetry books, a blurry future,
old debts, new intuitions, as if it all adds up,
composes a self hiding inside a lumpy body.
Being accumulates. What holds it together?
Time. Its restless interrogation of materials—
morning coffee, black grand pianos, red roses,
et cetera, et cetera—and then a dogpiling
of moods. The slow conflation of thoughts.
Look! I can install the moon to hang above
these lines even though it is morning as I sit
writing this all down, thinking, gawd, no more
traumas. Death, death. More dark coffee. Me
an unreliable narrator, or a holy pilgrim, or
an interloper hiding inside a fifty-year-old body,
waiting for a sparrow to bend a black branch
with its weight, or a jack-in-the-box full of
Chinese firecrackers to unspring itself. Things—
yes, things!—to break up the routine of
breathing in and out, which is my way of saying
I sing the body eclectic (sorry Uncle Walt), and
so do you, so let's form a choir of voices, then
pick each other's brains until questions surface:
Where do we go from here? Are waterfalls rivers
attempting suicide? Is poetry any good at all?
The answers we place in a box on a back shelf
buried in an evidence room. The cases officially
unsolved, and still the leads come pouring in.

Mirror Ball

A seven-year-old boy, chased by twin girls
with blonde hair, French braids, falls into tall grass
where they kiss his cheeks. Then he stands up
a teenager, and the twin girls are nowhere.
The mirror ball of time revolves until the boy
is a man with children of his own. I don't
know anything except these fragments of
light playing against the walls I call home.
Oh, and music! The various songs I attach
significance to resurrected in my thoughts.
"That's Entertainment." "Jane Says." "Where Is My Mind?"
The soundtrack of a life where I place
what at the centre? The red stripe of
a garter snake? A floating diving dock
buoyed in a small Muskoka lake all summer?
Out of darkness, out of the cave of breath,
comes the play of images, in pieces, what
once wove themselves into hours and days
spent folding hoses in a Goodyear factory
during an endless night shift, or hunting
grouse with a father cold autumn mornings.
The mirror ball spins. A GI Joe action figure
is missing an arm. A girl is showing her breasts
for the first time. Childhood, adulthood,
diamonding. I don't know when I may die,
or if my children will find comfort in these words,
or any other myriad things, but I know
this: the mirror ball of time spins, the music
plays, and the time for dancing is now.

New Epoch

We will speak the language of weak

and strong. We will stand in our living

rooms watching TV news, our shoes

no longer filling with blood. We will

be happy, risking it all, that happiness

at every turn. We will age gracefully

amidst machines. We will no longer

be overwhelmed by the sense portals.

Beauty will be the deep state. We will

be more than an amalgam of hurts.

We will live each day like a revelation,

inhabiting the world, no longer afraid.

We will migrate toward neighbours,

not celebrities. We will write fiery

messages of love and forgiveness.

We will worry less about real estate,

more about the sudden proliferation

of hurricanes. We will argue magic

is our birthright. We will make love

to science, not hurtful old stories.

We will get lost in meaning. We will

wake from heartache. We will run

for our lives, sharing the spotlight

at the ticker-tape finish. We will

marry ourselves to matter, divorce

any guilts. We will be the song we

sing, a melody of chemicals. We will

be a kingdom of nouns. A burning

effigy of verbs. We will be the echo,

the voices unbuttoning the future.

Left of the Dial

Whoever reads this, know I am not really here.
I am playing the Replacements' *Tim* on vinyl,
a band who flirted with immortality, simultaneously
giving it the finger. I loved rock 'n' roll before
it became about branding, T-shirts, Coachella.
My friends loaned me the first Violent Femmes
record. I heard brushed snares, nasally vocals,
guitar riffs as a pure feat of engineering genius.
I saw them once play the Concert Hall in 1991.
That is where I am right now if you're looking
for me. I am the tall lanky kid in the centre balcony
who has taken his brother there for his birthday.
Life is not a concert. A cacophony of Marshall
stacks, ear-splitting noise, a singer stepping up
to a microphone scream-singing "Add it up," but
it should be. How much is a life like that worth?
The songs keep piling up like the years, each with
their own signature chaos. Bad Brains covering
"Kick Out the Jams" or the Damned singing
"Smash It Up" or Hüsker Dü's *Candy Apple Grey*.
The imperfections in those songs make you feel
cooler than you have any right to be. That is why
suddenly I am sixteen once again watching
a video for the song "Left of the Dial,"
a stereo speaker thumping away in black and white,
the entire thing one continuous shot that feels
unfinished but perfect, in the way a poem can
feel unfinished, also perfect, and wholly enough.

Gallows

You sign up for eight years of university,
but not this torture on simmer. Changing
light bulbs. Going to the mall. Strangers
wanting to sell you things at your front
door. Grey skies in November. Parasites
growing in garbage. Fruit flies orbiting
a bowl of bananas. Try the sparkling water!
A hint of citrus goes well with dress-down
Fridays. The seesaw of aspirations versus
obligations. Get a massage. Read the days
inside out. Make it new. Write your own
secret chapter. A few words to compliment
your sale-rack nerves. Your pay-it-forward sadness.
Touch wood for the forests are on fire.
Narcissism and climate change fistfight over
parking spaces at outlet stores. Say your name
then try not to think of every sad hamster
running circles in small plastic cages in
elementary schools. May your happiness
be made of 100% Egyptian cotton, quirky
metaphors. Not lottery tickets or Ativan.
The gallows were abolished so take the rope
from around your neck. Stop climbing
the stairs. It is impolite to stare at your
executioner. When the trap door opens,
grow wings. That is the only way to disperse
a crowd. To know you are really alive.

Chardonnay

Liquid manna in a glass. Hints of green apple
or lemon zest, clover honey or grapefruit,
I admit I miss it. I was a lousy drunk, though.
I have no stomach for the morning after,
refusing to chase horror with another
round. I feel bad for those guys holding
signs panhandling for money across
from liquor stores, wanting to get enough
money together to buy a tallboy or a cheap
bottle of red. They are like living shipwrecks.
The flotsam of their lives usually a couple of
bags strewn around them. Maybe a black Lab
on a rope leash. Their dedication to suffering
complete. Recovery is a violent wind, what
buffets against an individual, and you have
to stand it every day, as it shakes and clangs
the cracked iron bell of your heart. Sobriety
is an awakening and a theft. A dividing
line between then and now. Guilt wringing
out the spirit, or the spirit wringing out
guilt. Fatalism needs to be folded carefully
into a drawer. Most days, I study my face
like a lost and found to see what has changed.
When people fiddle with wineglasses,
it makes me uncomfortable. The not drinking
makes life all the more poignant, and hard.
It frees you from a certain kind of pain, but
leaves you isolated and bereft if you let it.
I used to hold a glass of Chardonnay carefully
up to the light to note its colour and age.
It is much harder to do that with oneself.

Throw away the tasting notes. Interpret
the qualities of every day on your own,
love, loss, smells, taste, silence, seasons,
for this is your job now. This is your task.

Out of the Loop

I am the first-born son but the family fortune
was squandered on groceries years ago.
Old white men are yelling angrily on television
even though they own everything. The cords
in my hand are quietly pulling my fingers
down into a fist. Every writer I know
talks about CanLit but guffaws when
you mention Canada or maple syrup or blackflies
or dying northern Ontario Lakes.
Canada is the swampiest country I know!
My American poet friends are always writing
about America, or about dead poets
who wrote eloquently about America,
but try doing that with Canada,
and tongues start wagging. CanLit
is a giant potluck where everyone brought
knives and no one thought of any food.
I used to believe in CanLit. I travelled
to Drumheller and the high Arctic,
believing I would write the great Canadian poem,
but Canada doesn't need poems, it turns out.
We are fine with coffee and donuts,
another Saturday spent at the local rink.
The most a writer can hope for in our country
is to have a bench dedicated to them
beside a playground frequented by children
and old people, which is no small feat.
Look at my mighty works and despair!
I think of Milton, blind, making his daughters
take dictation and wonder how he'd fare
during a Canadian winter. Or Wordsworth

canoeing in Algonquin Park. Would he write
epic moose poems? Drown? The only way
a Canadian poet can get a dram of immortality—
something I would gladly drink if it had a hint of
caffeine. The promise of another arts grant.
O Canada, I love your muskeg kisses and grizzly
bear hugs! This is the only poem I will ever write you.
It will erect no statues. Please be gentle with it.

Mission Statement

I had trouble sleeping so I wrote a lullaby
called "Theories of Consciousness and Death."
I used the word *aubade* extravagantly like
a personal brand. My mission statement
for the next year is not worrying about life's
particulars. Approaching fifty is like waltzing
in traffic. My dance partner is beautiful.
One day my children will mourn my loss.
Until then, I am going to keep my ego
at half-mast and pull over for ambulances.
Listen to rain on the roof. The wind's
ailments. Hope, a Mylar balloon, slowly
floating along a schoolyard fence. Aging
has little to do with technique, so fake it.
My friends believe in art and metaphysics
even if these sections in mall bookstores
are scented candles. I want to say it doesn't
matter. I want to say it's not true. It's none
of my business but really we should stop
making small talk and write a requiem
for the middle class. Is there anything
sadder than self-checkout at the grocery
store? I am approaching my sixth decade
so where is my gift bag? There are less
and less days ahead and still something
in the immanent distance. Literature is
a corpse, or so my high school students
tell me. I reanimate dystopian nightmares.
The kids cheat on small quizzes. I ask if
they remember being five years old,
summer lasting forever? Wear that feeling

like a crown and the kingdom is yours.
If I was their age, I wouldn't believe it either.
The experts tell me I'm doing a great job
when really I would like to forget everything—
green grass, computer glitches, TV sitcoms—
so the world might rewrite its origin story,
something to do with *In the beginning...*
But it's been love at first sight for as long
as I can remember. This is my testimony
even if it is written in disappearing ink.

Fault Lines

Hate should be put on a diet. In between
ordinary and ecstasy is a matter of degrees.
My fault lines are growing more pronounced
without any seismic shifting. Trees in the yard
have roots planted in the last century. Pilgrimages
are no longer in style, but worshipping distraction is.
Illumination is a television screen. No one needs
a permit to write lies or promises. I am early
for my retirement party. My one contribution
to history is I often stare at the night sky.
I frame my insecurities. Hang them from a nail
I drive into every single day. This living is less
Victorian gardens, and more a never-ending
monologue of strangeness. We need a moratorium
on the inconsequential. The afterlife has been
oversold. No returns after midnight. Nothing
occupies the mind like the voices of addiction.
The fluorescent glow of the ego. Truth is rhythm.
Not stories the past sells you. I go fact-free for Lent,
but real thoughts keep getting in the way.
A river's meanderings are meaningless until it hits
a cliff. Then its swan dive is postcard-worthy.
The same cannot be said of human beings.
Good manners will not save us from despair,
but I place a napkin on my lap anyways.
Keep faith with language, no matter how plain,
and the rewards will be handwritten notes
reminding you who and what you are. A user
manual of self-loathing and forgiveness
providing little protection against
the moment crushing against your chest
whispering *new, new, new.*

Point of Entry

Nothing frou-frou. Maybe a thin veneer
of syllables evoking childhood days.
Maybe a confession to minor crimes:
not liking fruit yogurt, or clenching
one's fists when the plane is rocked by
turbulence. All my transcripts are blank,
which means I have a graduate degree
in possibilities, not conclusions. See?
My point of entry is making you smile.
To make you feel like you are in on the joke,
even if the joke says *Knock knock*,
then runs to the other side of a bridge
on fire. Some people treat poems
like pressed flowers in ancient books
when really it should be an uncovering.
Like lifting up an overturned bucket
in snow, and finding the grass still
green under there. It's all that under-
nothing that I am after. The sublime
is my favourite ringtone, but the calls
are less frequent than I would like.
As for an ending, I set fire to that, too.
Breaking out the medieval torture devices
is fine by me since being stretched
on a rack sounds a lot better than
being impaled by clarity. When
the torturer says *Had enough?* admit
your complicity. Say it all started
in grade school with haikus and games
of tag. Ready? You're it.

The Tail Wags the Comet

I have ashes in my mouth

from breathing fire. Sex

steeps desire in a Pangaea

of bodies. Hope has been

kidnapped but no one will

pay the ransom. A smidge

of magic is better than breaking

rocks in a prison yard. All

the guards are on the take.

My shiv is made of one word—

without. I stick it into the air

hoping to punish the world

for birthing me, which is like

the tail wagging the comet.

The truth is I want my soul

to ride through the car wash

with the top down. I'm trying

hard to not make this an elegy.

Writing about language and

memory is stanning for ghosts.

Please join my anonymous fan club.

There is a newsletter and a free

button stating *The world is ending.*

We can wear them in solidarity

when the flower shops close down,

which is the closest we will ever

get to being each other. You me

or me you, or we us. Together

a mob ready to turn on anyone

who mentions we live apart.

True or False

It was when I gave my keynote speech to the rain
that I went on my desert sabbatical. Where does
one trade in an angry soul? I get inside my car
to drive around town, watching people enter/
leave coffee shops, pharmacies, grocery stores,
everyone in a hurry, staring at phones, red lights,
green lights, no one dancing in public, arguing
about angels or demons. No unclaimed space
anywhere, which is why I have a fascination
with secret knowledge, the kind we keep mothballed,
do not share with anyone except under duress,
or in poems, like my belief I will come back
as an apple tree, or as a grasshopper, or as Li Bai
after I die which is strange when you think
I do not speak Chinese. However, I do have a great love
for the moon! I would migrate but to where?
All places are concrete and speed bumps and politics.
Sometimes I sway a little when my anxiety ramps up.
I moan under my breath. That is how I know
I am human and alive. Years ago, in a classroom
a voice entered me but it took years to tame it.
What's true or false? All the bridges in my town
seem lonely and suffering. I'm voting for fish, rivers,
fields, trees, all the things! Too bad
my ballot is spoiled. I pray my daughter's freckles
linger into adolescence. I pray my son's smile
outlasts his childhood. I want to fleece my memories
after spending a lifetime wearing these years,
praising, grieving, burning inside them.

Replicants

Diet Coke is more famous than Coleridge.
The sublime or Splenda? Am I a robot?
A replicant with synthesized tastes? Romantic poets
sit next to each other on dusty bookshelves.
Dreams of immortality seem quaint next to Instagram fame.
My imagination tells me I am five years old.
Thirty-five years old. Maybe fifty years old. I want back
a world where a stack of *National Geographics*
sits in every living room. I thought adulthood
would have more quicksand. Secret passageways.
Somewhere in the Bureau of Missing Persons,
a detective is looking over your file.
There are old yearbook pictures, a prom date.
One of you holding a large fish.
I don't have the heart to tell him the culprit
is time passing. This is not a prayer.
Stop catechizing disappointments and sorrows.
Throw out the boomerang of hope. The parachute fits.
The falling airplane is invisible. Secrets multiply
in church basements every day of the week.
I want the secret beyond the secret. How to live,
how to die with dignity. Without bending a knee
or kowtowing to religion. The rhododendrons
are drunk on colours! They love themselves
with a feverish abandon so why can't I? I would say
enough is enough but it wouldn't be true. If only
wild apprehension would declare a ceasefire
long enough for me to enjoy another sci-fi movie.
I've seen things you people wouldn't believe,
says Roy Batty in *Blade Runner* before dying in the rain.
It only took me this long in life to believe him.

Antennae

I like the feeling of the fine hairs on my arm
standing on end, which happens every time
I think about certain poems arrowing into my heart,
or why the birds keep singing every morning
when clearly their lives are more difficult than mine,
or the gentle laughter of my friend Adam
telling a story about shooting heroin in his truck
on the way home from a long shift at the Ford factory.
I remember my last hangover. Adam saying
he would drive out to meet me at my dad's house,
that he wasn't doing hard drugs, only "drinking
a few beers with the boys." That he is gone
and I am still here leaves me wanting to understand
more than ever what this living is, its rooms of
rain and élan, as I imagine the opiates
arrowing through his heart one last time.
I wish I could tell him sobriety finely attunes
the downy antennae of your arm hairs,
making them stand on end when life really
kicks into high gear which if you ask me
has to do with the smell of my girlfriend's hair,
explaining *Hamlet* to my students,
takeout Thai food, bright full moons
that make me feel like 90% fallen star, 10% a man
who survived rehab, who survived it all,
my dumb luck shining in the dark.

My Life in Art

I stand before this canvas which is really
only blue skies, a couple small birds
attacking a crow, and I wonder where
I misplaced my easel? I'm a so-so artist.
I had my own blue period. I sabotage
sketches by mixing in words instead of
paints. To this day, I forget who is the god
of not giving a fuck. I'm a cheerleader for
underdogs, nudes in paintings. Sadly,
my artist friends only paint portraits, some
watercolours, which is too bad given nudity
is the best subject matter for paintings, and
real life, even if we pretend we are not naked
under these clothes. The way to communicate
is with the eyes, which has something to do
with art and sex and feelings. I'm always trying
to get to the other side of the canvas or the page
or your body depending on what I'm looking at.
This is a terrible painting. I have not even added
the bee stings, or the bruises, or the Garden
of Earthly Office Parties yet. Go easy with
your critique but tell me the truth. You look
a little sad in your clothes. Let's get naked
while the paint dries. C'mon, I'll go first.

Once More for the People in the Back

Books are my morphine. Ditto the sun. If night is secular,
why do I seek its blessing? I'd rather build a paper kingdom
then bend a knee, or kiss anyone's ring. Words are joiners.
They connect to everything, inexactly, like how oil paints
connect the naked young model, half-shrouded in a white
bedsheet, to the artist in the chilly airless room. I say
Anything, anything, under my breath like a hymn. Whose
century is this? Too early to tell. My muse is a bricked-up
window. A phone booth with its cord cut. My ardent wish
is that a little wisdom will tempt you to let go of your caution
before the cavalry arrives too late. Before the rain sulks,
ruining the wedding. Hope is rapacious. You can't bottle up
lyricism. We drink its contents thirsty for what is new.
I like to think of myself as a prodigy of serial monogamy.
Sometimes the right phrase shines through. To where?
It's a toss-up between a dark forest circling my childhood,
and a forgotten shopping mall full of people seeking escape.
No ideas but in brand clothing, says the mall's directory.
Who is going to do our dirty work? Hackneyed little men
are always willing to put up grubby little hands. The afterlife
is no longer taking reservations so try farther down the street.
Billions of stars, and not one of them hears us down here
squabbling over physics, low-income housing, this sonnet
which is not a sonnet but a riot of voltas. I'm picketing
for enlightenment over lobotomies. Really, I would like nothing
more than to listen to you read just three more sad poems
after anaesthetizing a local crowd seated at small candlelit tables,
but look! There is a field of dandelions all losing their minds,
in unison! A dorm-room kid is saying *I love you* in the dark!
Wonder biopsied is still wonder. Without any irritable reaching after facts,
I dare you to look at a rose bush. Connect these dots.

High-five

When the world makes you cry uncle,
try high-fiving random strangers,
or building ice sculptures to look
like poets who died too young.
Run a marathon. Take an Italian
cooking class. Start birdwatching.
Yes, things are bad, but at least
most of us will never have to perform
a high-wire act or walk on hot coals.
Try thinking about a Scandinavian spa,
the first person you ever French kissed.
The taste of strawberries. It is easy to forget
the good cop's soothing voice in the corner
when the bad cop starts slapping you.
I guess what I am saying is we can be both
optimistic and scared, still gawk at sparrows
murmuring while waiting for the flood
to arrive. Two roads diverged in a …
blah, blah, blah. When the drummer quits,
maybe you have to stamp your feet.
The glass is half-empty, sure, but it is also filled
with WiFi, Maine Coon kittens, a night sky
filled with constellations. That some stars
are dead and have been for millennia
is no matter. That they still shine reminds me
I am in good shape, despite my being
a shape everything else isn't.

Acknowledgements

I am grateful to the editors of *Griffel*, *The Pi Review*, *The Malahat Review* and *Sonora Review* for first publishing some of these poems.

Thank you to my family and to my many friends who supported me while I pestered them with new poems, especially Paul Vermeersch, Jim Johnstone, Samuel Strathman and my favourite valentine Aura Hertzog.

I would especially like to thank Silas White and the whole crew at Nightwood Editions, as well as the staff and students at Bluevale Collegiate Institute who make me look forward to going to work.

Last of all, a big hug to Percy, Noah, Olivia and Elliot for being terrific kids!

About the Author

Chris Banks is a Canadian poet and author of six collections of poems, most recently *Deepfake Serenade* from Nightwood Editions (2021). His first full-length collection, *Bonfires*, was awarded the Jack Chalmers Award for poetry by the Canadian Authors' Association in 2004, and was also a finalist for the Gerald Lampert Memorial Award for best first book of poetry in Canada. His poetry has appeared in *The New Quarterly, Arc Poetry Magazine, The Antigonish Review, Event, The Malahat Review, Griffel, American Poetry Journal* and *Prism International*, among other publications. He lives and writes in Kitchener, Ontario.